BELIEVE HIS PROPHETS & PRO$PER

D'ARCY G. RABOTEAU

"Posted!" III
BELIEVE HIS PROPHETS & PRO$PER

King James Version (KJV)
Public Domain
Amplified Bible (AMP)
Copyright © 2015 by The Lockman Foundation, La Habra, CA 90631. All rights reserved.

The views expressed in this work are solely those of the author and do not necessarily reflect the views of the publisher, and the publisher hereby disclaims any responsibility for them.

iUniverse books may be ordered through booksellers or by contacting:

iUniverse
1663 Liberty Drive
Bloomington, IN 47403
www.iuniverse.com
1-800-Authors (1-800-288-4677)

Because of the dynamic nature of the Internet, any web addresses or links contained in this book may have changed since publication and may no longer be valid. The views expressed in this work are solely those of the author and do not necessarily reflect the views of the publisher, and the publisher hereby disclaims any responsibility for them.

Any people depicted in stock imagery provided by Getty Images are models, and such images are being used for illustrative purposes only. Certain stock imagery © Getty Images.

ISBN: 978-1-5320-6314-5 (sc)
ISBN: 978-1-5320-6315-2 (e)

Library of Congress Control Number: 2018910788

Print information available on the last page.

iUniverse rev. date: 12/21/2018

<u>To My New Friends On Facebook</u>

"Greater love has no man than this,
that a man lay down his life for his friends.
You are my friends, if you do whatever I command you…
for all things that I have heard of my Father
I have made known to you."
(John 15:13-15)

"This is the covenant that I will make with them after those days,
says the Lord, I will put My laws into their hearts,
and in their minds I will write them."
(Hebrews 10:16)

CONTENTS

SPECIAL FEATURES

INTRODUCTION

"Believe in the LORD your God, and you shall be established;
believe His prophets, and you shall prosper."
(2 Chronicles 20:20)

Several years ago, I was teaching at a financial seminar in my former church where I stood [in the spirit of King Jehoshaphat] and boldly declared to the congregation: *"Your Prosperity Is Connected To God's Prophets!"*, a revelation and principle that was inspired by the above scripture. And it's *this same "prophetic prosperity principle"* which is the foundation for the revelation in *this* book.

Although "in context", the word "prosper" in 2 Chronicles 20:20 wasn't *specifically* denoting "financial prosperity", but "in principle" it most certainly was. Proof of that is found in verse 25 in this same chapter where it says:

> *"And when Jehoshaphat and his people came to take away their*
> *spoil, they found among them an abundance of valuables on*
> *the dead bodies, and precious jewelry, which they stripped off*
> *for themselves, more than they could carry away; and they were*
> *three days gathering the spoil because there was so much."*

Here we can clearly see the "financial and material prosperity" of God's people post-battle. But more importantly, we can see how King Jehoshaphat's victory over his enemies was directly linked to believing and following the instructions of "His prophet!"

In general, the word "prosper" means: "to flourish, thrive, grow, do well, succeed, *and* make money". So by reason of this definition alone [not to mention the countless number of scriptures that support this truth--many of which are in *this* book], we can conclude that **God wants His people to "prosper" in every area of their lives including their finances.**

So why is it so important to *"believe His prophets"* as the scripture instructs us to do? And how can *your* decision [to *believe* or *not to believe*] "His prophets" impact *your* "financial prosperity?" Let's take a look at the following scenarios to help answer these questions:

❖ *If **Peter** had not decided to **"believe His prophet" (Jesus)**, then he would not have **"prospered"**...and known* that he could trust Jesus for his financial provision (Matthew 17:24-27).

In another instance with Peter and Jesus:

❖ *If **Peter** had not decided to **"believe His prophet" (Jesus)**, then he would not have **"prospered"**...and* he and his partner's boats would not have overflowed with nets of fish (Luke 5:1-11);

❖ *If **the widow at Zarephath** had not decided to **"believe His prophet" (Elijah)**, then she would not have **"prospered"**...and* she and her son would not have survived the famine (1 Kings 17:8-16);

❖ *If **the widow of one of the sons of the prophets** had not decided to **"believe His prophet" (Elisha)**, then she would not have **"prospered"**...and* her two sons would've been taken away as slaves to pay off her debt (2 Kings 4:1-7);

❖ *If **pharaoh** had not decided to **"believe His prophet" (Joseph)**, then he would not have **"prospered"**...and* he and the entire nation of Egypt would've suffered immensely and many people would've died of starvation during the severe famine (Genesis 41:14-57).

In the five examples I just mentioned (which only scratch the surface of many more similar examples throughout the Bible), *notice the link between "His prophets" and the "Supernatural provision and prosperity of His people".* In this volume, I will set the "prophetic prosperity principle" found in 2 Chronicles 20:20 in the life of Joseph, and then show you how *this* "principle" applies to *yours* and *my* "prosperity" today under the New Covenant.

There's a severe famine coming! But here's the good news: ***no famine affecting man ever has or ever will catch God by surprise, because He knows the past, present, and future of all things!*** Which means, God in His goodness will always provide a person, a nation, and its leaders with "the answers" to any major crises they will face *long before* the crises ever occurs, and He provides those "answers" through "His prophets!"

The Bible declares, *"Surely the LORD God does nothing, but He reveals His secrets to His servants the prophets." (Amos 3:7)* We can also see *this particular* "prophetic principle" active in the life of Joseph.

At God's appointed time, the Spirit of God moved *upon* Joseph and he not only "interpreted" pharaoh's dreams, but he took it a step further and *revealed* to pharaoh a "14-year strategy" (or, plan) that would save the nation of Egypt [and its surrounding nations] from the coming famine. This "Divinely inspired plan" by Joseph not only positioned Egypt to *survive* but to *thrive* throughout the famine.

And like Joseph, this is also how the Spirit of God is moving *in* and *upon* many of "His prophets" *in* "the Church" today!

As "believers", we have the opportunity and privilege to be on both the "receiving" and the "giving" side of this principle in 2 Chronicles 20:20. On the "receiving" side: it's important for each of us [as leaders and lay members] to *recognize* "His prophets" when they are "sent" to us, and then ***"believe His prophets"*** so we will *prosper.*

And on the "giving" side: it's equally important for us to understand that *God is now preparing and Supernaturally positioning "His servants the prophets" in the marketplace [like never before in these last days] to be the vessels He uses to pour out "His knowledge and wisdom" upon world leaders and industries during times of economic famine.*

Are *you* ready to be *poured into* at this appointed time, so that the Spirit of God can *pour you out* upon the nations? If so, then the "revelation" in this book will position *you* to "receive" and "hear God's Voice" at another level, so that He'll be able to *pour you out* in the same capacity that *you* were *poured into! (Selah)*

On My Watch:
"The Conversations Continue"

This book picks up where *"Posted!" II, The Prophet's Watch* left off.

In fact, the "last Watchman Status" in volume two sets the stage for the "12 Watchman $tatuses" that are contained in this volume. So if you haven't read volume two yet, then I encourage you to grab a copy today and read it.

By the way, the number "12" is a *very significant number* in the scriptures because it symbolizes "governmental order and maturity". For example, we see the number "12" in:

- ❖ *the 12 tribes of Israel in the Old Testament;*
- ❖ *the 12 disciples/apostles of Christ in the New Testament;*
- ❖ *and the 12 gates/foundations described in the city of Heaven.*

We also see the number "12" revealed in:

- ❖ *the 120 years that God gave man to repent in Noah's day;*
- ❖ *and the 120 disciples who waited for and received the infilling of the Holy Spirit on the day of Pentecost.*

The number "12" represents "Divine order", *and* it establishes a new and strong foundation for "greater revelation and miracles".

In my former account, *"The Prophet's Watch"*, I was given a mandate to *"Watch, Write, and Wait for the vision"* according to Habakkuk 2:1-3. Well, *that* "prophetic mandate" still continues as I have written the vision on the twelve tablets in this volume, so that *you* may run that read them.

As you *meditate* and "receive the revelation" engraved upon these twelve tablets, I decree:

> *"Greater revelation and tangible miracles are coming into your life in this season, specifically in the area of your finances!"*

So expect:

* ❖ *Supernatural debt-cancellation,*
* ❖ *a new well-paying job offer in your field of expertise,*
* ❖ *a new promotion or raise that doubles your current salary,*
* ❖ *a new business idea or partnership that yields massive wealth for you and your partner(s),*
* ❖ *Divine favor through a specific person or relationship who's in a position to greatly bless you financially,*
* ❖ *Divine wisdom and strategy that quickly boosts product sales for your company and prevents employee downsizing,*
* ❖ *etc.*

Whatever *your specific miracle* is, I am believing and decreeing that **you're about to be launched into a new dimension of prosperity and wealth like never before in this season**...*And what God has for you, is exclusively for you!*

∿*The time is NOW to believe His prophets & prosper!*

Money "Answers" ALL Things

(Not Just SOME Things)!

"A feast is made for laughter, and wine makes merry,
*but **money answers all things**."*
(Ecclesiastes 10:19)

In order for money to "answer" a thing, then that means, money has a "voice". And according to this scripture, **the "voice" of money "answers" not just "some" things, but "ALL" things—which would include both "good" things and "bad" things. Money is neutral, so "whoever has the money" determines "how it's being used", or "what things" are being "answered" or not!**

Most people today don't even realize the *major role* that "money" plays in the manifestation of *evil* upon the Earth. *That,* **in order for the "works of the devil" to be manifested on the Earth, they must first be "financed by someone" on the Earth!**

And this same principle applies on the flip side of the coin. *That,* **in order for "works of righteousness by the Holy Spirit" to be manifested on the Earth, they too must first be "financed by someone" on the Earth!**

So does it really matter "who" has the majority of control over the money and wealth on the Earth?—you bet it does!—which is why "the devil" has always fought "the Church" from having total dominion over the money, wealth, and prosperity on the Earth! And why has he fought "the Church" so hard in the area of "money", including those whom God has called to preach the Gospel of pro$perity? Because "money" is what "the devil" has been holding "his anointing" on from day one, so that he can continue to "control" the nations and have "influence" over billions of lives [through mainstream media and the other major world kingdoms], none of which could be possible without "money!"

*The reality is, **"someone" has to be "the instrument that God uses" to underwrite "His Vision", which is the preaching of the Gospel in all nations, and the manifestation of His goodness in the lives of people upon the Earth**—just like **"someone" has to be "the instrument the devil uses" to underwrite "his vision", which is preaching against the Gospel [and those men and women who preach the Gospel], and the manifestation of evil and destruction in the lives of people upon the Earth!***

<u>*The question is:*</u>

*"Whose vision are YOU underwriting:
the devil's vision, or God's Vision?"*

As you honestly answer this question for yourself, *keep in mind that* **the real problem has never been with "the money", but with "the person" whose hands "the money" is in, and how "that person" has decided to use it!** *(Selah)* Money can either be used for "good" or for "evil", to *save* lives or to *destroy* them!

But the Bible's story of "Joseph" lets us know that **the Father has always had an uncommon plan to Supernaturally position "His servants the prophets" to be the "recipients and distributors of great wealth" for the preaching of the Gospel, for the work of the Lord, for**

**the advancement of God's Kingdom on Earth—and this will result
in the saving of many lives!**

"Money answers *all things"* no doubt! The question is: *What "things" are
YOU allowing **"your money"** to be an "answer" to on the Earth—"the
good works of God" that **save** lives, or "the works of the devil" that **destroy**
lives?*

∿ Scripture References:

- ➢ *Genesis 50:20*
- ➢ *Proverbs 13:22b*
- ➢ **Ecclesiastes 10:19**
- ➢ *John 10:10*

- ➢ *Acts 10:38*
- ➢ **1 Timothy 6:10,** *17-19*
- ➢ *1 John 3:8*

The Turning Point

Joseph was Supernaturally positioned to receive *"NEW levels of uncommon favor and wealth"* upon his life *not* while he was still at home in Canaan among his half-brethren, *but [only when] he was out of his comfort zone in a foreign land (Egypt) around foreign people using his God-given gifts to solve problems for people who were strangers. (Genesis 39-40)*

But ***"the turning point" came in Joseph's financial life when a "king" had a major problem that only Joseph could solve with his God-given gift!*** *(Genesis 41)*

Promotion comes from the LORD! *And it was **"the LORD"** who gave **"Joseph"** UNCOMMON FAVOR with **"the king"** and PROMOTED him to the esteemed position of Prime Minister of Egypt, making Joseph a "steward over enormous amounts of wealth and resources" during a severe 7-year famine in the land!*

And like Joseph, I decree and declare that:

"A major turning point is NOW happening in your financial life in this season! And God is NOW opening palace doors and giving you UNCOMMON FAVOR with a king [in your field or industry] who has a major problem that only you can solve with your God-given gift(s) and talents!"

Now *you "declare"* it, and *"expect"* it to happen for *you* in this season!

∾ *Scripture References:*

- ➢ *Genesis 39-41*
- ➢ *Psalms 75:6-7*
- ➢ *Proverbs 18:16*

- ➢ *Matthew 25:14-23*
- ➢ *Hebrews 13:1-2*

"The Tithing Generation And The Mantle Of A True Tither!"

*"You are cursed with a curse, for you have robbed Me, even this whole nation...[**But here's how you reverse the curse and release the Blessing:] Bring all the tithes into the storehouse, so that there may be meat in My house,** and prove Me now in this', says the LORD of hosts, 'if I will not open for you the windows of heaven and pour you out [the Blessing], that there will not be room enough to receive it."*
(Malachi 3:9-10)

<u>As I stand upon my watch, I see:</u>

"A nation and generation of young people who are saved and filled with the Holy Spirit AND who have been taught and trained in the principles of Kingdom Economics (such as tithing) as a way of life!...

<u>I see:</u>

~ **Young tither$** *who faithfully sow 10% of their gross income into the Lord's work, and who know how to put a demand on their covenant with God!...*
(Malachi 3:10-12)

6

∽ *Young tither$ who are not greedy of filthy lucre, but who honor the LORD with their income (money) and with the first-fruits of ALL their increase, which causes their houses [and bank accounts] to be filled with wealth & riches, and their businesses to overflow with NEW money!...*
(Proverbs 3:9-10)

∽ *Young tither$ who personally know God as Jehovah-Jireh, their One true $ource, and [through their sacrificial sowing of $EED into the anointing], God [Supernaturally] provides for them in spite of opposing circumstances!...*
(Genesis 22:1-18)

∽ *Young tither$ whom God has given power to get wealth through multiple streams of income, and they tithe systematically and faithfully off of every one of them!"*
(Genesis 2:10-14; Deuteronomy 8:18)

Keep in mind that **"these young tither$"** are *not* just *young* according to their natural age, but [despite their *age* in the natural] these **"are the ones whom the Father has given me to teach and train up in the revelation knowledge and principles that make up the mantle that He has placed upon my life as a true tither!"**

Therefore, in light of this revelation, and in obedience to my Father:

*"I NOW release a double-portion of **my MANTLE as a TRUE TITHER** upon these young tither$ whom the Father has given me to partake in my revelation and anointing!"*

*And **I PROPHE$Y** over these **young tither$**, that:*

"The windows of heaven are NOW open over you and God is NOW pouring out The Blessing (of Abraham) upon your life [and upon your finances], that there will not be room enough to receive it!"
(Malachi 3:10)

"God is NOW rebuking the devourer for your sake, so that he will not destroy (or, corrupt) the fruits of your ground, neither will the vine fail to bear fruit for you in your field!"
(Malachi 3:11)

"All nations NOW call you 'Blessed', because you are 'a blessing' to all nations, and you are a delightful land!"
(Malachi 3:12)

Furthermore, **I PROPHE$Y** *over these* **young tither$**, *that:*

"You will remember the LORD your God, for it He who gives you power to get wealth, so that He may establish (launch) His covenant which He promised to your forefathers, as it is this day!"
(Deuteronomy 8:18)

"Your special gifts (talents and abilities) are NOW making room for you and bringing you before great men and women!"
(Proverbs 18:16; Matthew 25:14-23)

"Witty inventions and creative [money-making] ideas are NOW being fully developed and birthed through your hands into the marketplace for a profit!"
(Deuteronomy 28:8, 12; Proverbs 8:12; Isaiah 48:17)

"You are a successful entrepreneur, and you NOW own and oversee several very lucrative Kingdom businesses that are all prospering right in the midst of a collapsing world economy!"
(2 Kings 4:1-7)

"The Blessing of the LORD it NOW makes you rich, and He adds no sorrow with it!"
(Proverbs 10:22)

"Wealth and riches are NOW in your house(es), [in your hands, and in your bank accounts], and your righteousness endures forever!"
(Psalms 112:3)

*"The curse of poverty is NOW completely broken off your life,
and the Blessing of Abraham (God's covenant of wealth & riches)
is NOW completely evident upon you and your family!"*
(Genesis 13:2; 24:35; Galatians 3:13-14)

*"The wealth of the wicked is NOW being Supernaturally
transferred into your hands and your bank accounts for
Kingdom building and expansion on Earth!"*
(Genesis 41:37-57; Exodus 12:35-36; Proverbs 13:22b)

*"God is NOW causing men and women from every nation
to give money (wealth) into your bosom— good measure,
pressed down, shaken together, and running over!"*
(Luke 6:38)

*"You are NOW living a debt-free lifestyle of abundance,
owing no man nothing but to love him!"*
(John 10:10b; Romans 13:8)

And finally, **I PROPHE$Y** *over these* **young tither$**, *that:*

*"You are a chosen generation, a royal priesthood, a Holy nation, a
peculiar people of* **TRUE TITHER$ & MULTIMILLIONAIRE$**—
*for the preaching of the Gospel, for the work of the Lord,
for the advancement of God's Kingdom on Earth!"*

∿*My* **MANTLE** *as a* **TRUE TITHER** *has NOW been released…
will* **you** *receive it and walk in it today!?*

∿Scripture References:

➤ *Genesis 14:17-24*
➤ *2 Kings 2:8-15*
➤ *Malachi 3:10-12*

➤ *John 4:23-24*
➤ *2 Corinthians 9:6-15*
➤ *Ephesians 3:20*

9

First Generation TITHER$

> *"Then Melchizedek king of Salem brought out bread and wine;*
> *he was the priest of God Most High. And he blessed him and said:*
> *'Blessed be Abram of God Most High, Possessor of heaven and earth;*
> *and blessed be God Most High, Who has delivered your enemies into*
> *your hand.'* ***And he gave him a 'tithe' of all.***" *(Genesis 14:18-20)*

"Are *you* a first generation tither?" If *your parents or grandparents were not* "tithers", but *you are* a "tither" today, then yes, *you* most certainly *are* "a first generation tither!"

Foundation for Pro$perity. Now why is the question of being a "first generation tither" (or not) such an important question to ask and even more important to answer? *Because* ***"first generation tithers" lay a strong financial foundation for "their children and grandchildren"*** *(second and third generation tithers)* ***to build upon, so that they can walk in even greater levels of prosperity and wealth than that of their parents and grandparents!***

This *financial foundation* causes *"second and third generation tithers"* to already have an advantage over their peers, which also empowers them to be many *steps ahead* in their finances *and* in life. This is the result of *"their parents"* having already *gone ahead* and *paved the way* for their children to walk in *"the Blessing"* on their lives through *"tithing!"*

My CRO$$. It has been *my personal experience as a **"first generation tither"*** that I've had to *walk through hell* while *standing on God's Word against all kinds of [generational] "poverty demons" (principalities and powers)*…just so that *"Christ" [through me]* could "redeem" *me and my family* from the *[generational] "curse of poverty", being made a curse for us (for it is written, "Cursed is everyone who hangs on a tree"),* so that the *[generational]* ***"Blessing of Abraham"*** can come upon *me and my family* through Jesus Christ, so that *we* might receive the *"promise of true wealth and riches"* through faith!

Over the years [as a born again, Spirit-filled believer] I've made *many* ***"major financial sacrifices" [in $EED-sowing** and **in the voluntary release of specific material possessions** and **income channels]*** *all of which were done in obedience to God's Voice.* This is in addition to *many* ***"transitional financial setbacks"*** I've personally had to endure which were related to those ***"major financial sacrifices".*** Understand that I experienced those *"financial setbacks"* not because I *wasn't* "tithing", but because I *was* "tithing" on a consistent basis, and *my* "tithes and offerings" was *my* "$EED" that God was using to *establish a strong foundation* for *me and my family* to prosper in the future!

Growing in the Grace. By the grace of God *"I AM a true tither",* and I have been *"tithing" consistently* for nearly twenty years. Although *"tithing"* is a *"special grace" (anointing)* upon my life that I can take no credit for, I still had to do the work ***in order for me to "grow in this grace" over the years. In other words, I had to choose to remain faithful and continue to "tithe" even in the face of financial adversity so that "the Blessing" could be manifested upon my life at new levels!***

Tither$ Salute! I thank God for *my father-in-the-Gospel* who was the first to introduce me to "prosperity principles" on *"tithing"* many years ago, which helped to *lay the foundation* for "revelation knowledge" the Spirit of God has continued to give me over the years as a *"tither!"*

To every *"**first generation tither**"* out there—*I salute you* for *"laying the foundation"*, and for *"passing down your mantle as a tither"* to the *"next generation of tithers"* after you!

And to every *"**second and third generation tither**"* out there—*I salute you too* for *"receiving and walking in the tither's mantle passed down to you from your forefathers"*, so that *"the Blessing"* that comes through *"tithing"* will continue on from generation to generation!!!

∼*Scripture References:*

- ➢ *Genesis 14:20 (Abram)*
- ➢ *Deuteronomy 8:18*
- ➢ *2 Kings 2:8-15*
- ➢ *Jeremiah 29:11*
- ➢ *Malachi 3:10-12 (Israel)*

- ➢ *Mark 10:29-31*
- ➢ *1 Corinthians 15:10*
- ➢ *2 Corinthians 8:7, 9*
- ➢ *Galatians 3:13-14*
- ➢ *Ephesians 6:12*

Heaven's Marketing $trategy

The *"best marketing strategy"* you could ever have for *"your business"* is *"God's favor!"* But in order for you to have *"God's favor"* on *"your business"*, you must first *"apply His principles!"*

Application of God's principles = "favor" with God & man,

and "favor" with God & man = prosperity (wealth, abundance).

When "God's favor" is on "your business" soon everyone will hear about you, and many people will rush to pay any amount to purchase "your products, goods, and services!"

Secular marketing strategies that include *investing* and *networking* serve only as *a means to an end* when *"God's favor"* is on *"your business"*.

In order to prosper in the Kingdom of God (whether it's in business or in another field), the first thing you must do is "partner up with God's Word and principles and then focus on following His instructions!"

Do *whatever* "He" tells you to do! So if "He" tells you to *invest*, then invest…If "He" tells you to *network*, then network…If "He" tells you to *partner and do business with someone in particular who's trustworthy,* then do it!

And when you *follow the specific instructions* that "He" gives to you directly or through one of "His prophets", then watch *"His favor and financial blessings"* come *rushing* upon *"you"* and *"your business!"*

<u>*Jesus said it this way:*</u>

> *"But seek first the Kingdom of God and His righteousness, and all these things shall be ADDED to you." (Matthew 6:33)*

∽ *Scripture References:*

- ➤ *Deuteronomy 28:1-14*
- ➤ *2 Kings 4:7*
- ➤ *Proverbs 3:3-4; 8:12*
- ➤ *Isaiah 48:17*

- ➤ *Matthew 25:14-30*
- ➤ *Luke 5:1-11; 16:1-13*
- ➤ *Romans 12:2*

31 Pro$perity Scriptures
For Daily Meditation

Everyone loves a new challenge from time to time, right? Certainly *God* loves new challenges! And because *man* was created *"in His image and after His likeness"*, **we should also embrace new challenges—especially those that require us to exercise our faith and push us into new levels of success!**

In light of this, I've got a *NEW financial challenge* for you! Don't worry, it doesn't require you to spend any of *your money,* but it will require you to spend a little bit of *your time!* If you're interested, then here it is:

> *"I want to challenge you to MEDITATE on the following scriptures every day and night (according to Joshua 1:8) for THIRTY-ONE DAYS STRAIGHT at the beginning of each new month—for then you will make your way PRO$PEROU$, and then you will have good $UCCE$$!"*

To *"meditate"* means: *"to contemplate or intentionally think on something over and over again in your mind"*; it could be a specific thought, idea, concept, etc.

In like manner, **"scriptural meditation"** means: *"to contemplate or intentionally think on **the Word of God** over and over again in your* *mind"*; it is agreeing or siding with **God's "written" Word** so that you may observe to do [or, act in correspondence with] it.

The following are thirty-one of *my* favorite *"financial prosperity scriptures"* in the Bible that I "meditate" on every day, so consider *me* right there doing *this challenge* with *you!*

As your personal prosperity coach for this challenge, I want you not only to "read" the scriptures but to *"meditate"*, *"appropriate"*, and *"see yourself" in the scriptures*. **See yourself as Adam, Abraham, Isaac, Jacob, Joseph, Moses, Joshua, Ruth, David, Solomon, etc.—see yourself as the one whom God is blessing right NOW, both financially and materially!**

And *as we both come into "agreement" with these prosperity scriptures (according to Matthew 18:19)*, I am believing God for *"tremendous financial miracles and breakthroughs"* to be birthed through *your life* and *mine!*

And again, don't just STOP after completing one month—simply *repeat the same process (or, work this same prosperity system)* month after month for the entire year! For beginners: you can meditate on "one new scripture a day" in sequence over a 31-day period, until you graduate to meditating on "all 31 scriptures" each day!

Now if you're ready to accept *this new challenge*, then *let's get started…* as you "renew your mind to the Word of God" and position yourself for *Divine prosperity and success!*

1. **GENESIS 2:10-12** – *"Now a river went out of Eden to water the garden, and from there it parted and became four riverheads.*

   *The name of the first is Pishon; it is the one which skirts the whole land of Havilah, where there is **gold**. And **the gold of that land is good**. **Bdellium** and **the onyx stone** are there."*

2. <u>**GENESIS 13:2**</u> – *"And Abram was **very rich** in **cattle,** in **silver,** and in **gold.**"*

3. <u>**GENESIS 13:14-17**</u> – *"And the LORD said to Abram, after Lot had separated from him: "Lift your eyes now and look from the place where you are—northward, southward, eastward, and westward; for **all the land** which **you see** I give **to you** and **your descendants forever**…Arise, walk in **the land** through its length and its width, for I give it to you."*

4. <u>**GENESIS 24:35**</u> – *"And the LORD has **blessed** my master (Abraham) greatly; and he is become **great**. And He has given him **flocks,** and **herds,** and **silver,** and **gold,** and **menservants,** and **maidservants,** and **camels,** and **asses.**"*

5. <u>**GENESIS 26:12-14**</u> – *"Then Isaac **sowed** in that land, and received in the same year **a hundredfold,** and the LORD **blessed** him.*

   *And the man became **great,** and went forward, and **grew** until he became **very great.***

   *For he had **possession of flocks,** and **possession of herds,** and **great store of servants,** and the Philistines envied him."*

6. <u>**GENESIS 30:43**</u> – *"And the man (Jacob) **increased exceedingly,** and had **much cattle,** and **maidservants,** and **menservants,** and **camels,** and **asses.**"*

7. <u>**GENESIS 41:39-43**</u> – *"Then Pharaoh said to Joseph, 'Inasmuch as **God has shown you all this,** there is no one as **discerning** and **wise** as you. **You shall be over (in charge of) my house,** and **all my people shall be ruled according to your word;** only in regard to the throne will I be greater than you.'*

*And Pharaoh said to Joseph, 'See, I have set you **over all the land of Egypt**.'*

*Then Pharaoh took **his signet ring** off his hand and put it on Joseph's hand; and he clothed him in **garments of fine linen** and put **a gold chain** around his neck. And he made him ride in **the second chariot** which he had (symbolizing that Joseph was **second in command/power/authority** under Pharaoh); and they cried out before him, 'Bow the knee!'*

*So he set him over **all the land of Egypt**."*

8. **<u>EXODUS 3:21-22</u>** – *"And I will give this people **favor in the sight of the Egyptians,** and it shall come to pass that when you go, you shall not go empty-handed.*

    *But every woman shall borrow of her neighbor, and of her that dwells near her house, **jewels of silver,** and **jewels of gold,** and **clothing;** and you shall put them on your sons and on your daughters, **and you shall spoil (plunder) the Egyptians**."*

9. **<u>EXODUS 12:35</u>** – *"And the children of Israel did according to the word of Moses, and they borrowed of the Egyptians **jewels of silver,** and **jewels of gold,** and **clothing;***

    *And the LORD gave the people **favor in the sight of the Egyptians** so that they lent unto them such things as they required. **And they spoiled (plundered) the Egyptians**."*

10. **<u>DEUTERONOMY 8:18</u>** – *"But you shall remember the LORD your God: for it is He that gives you **power to get wealth,** so that He may establish His covenant which He promised to your forefathers, as it is this day."*

11. **<u>DEUTERONOMY 28:2-13</u>** – *"And **all these blessings** shall **come upon you** and **overtake you**, because you obey the Voice of the LORD your God:*

*You shall be **blessed in the city**, and you shall be **blessed in the country**.*

*You shall **be blessed in the fruit of your body**, the **produce of your ground** and the **increase** of your herds, the **increase of your cattle** and the **offspring of your flocks**.*

***Your basket** and **your kneading bowl** shall **be blessed**.*

*You shall be **blessed when you come in**, and you shall be **blessed when you go out**.*

*The LORD will **cause your enemies who rise against you to be defeated before your face**; they shall come out against you one way and flee before you seven ways.*

*The LORD will **command the blessing on you** in **your storehouses** and in **all to which you set your hand,** and He will **bless you** in **the land** which the LORD your God is giving you…*

*And the LORD will **grant you plenty of goods**, in the **fruit of your body**, in the **increase of your livestock**, and in **the produce of your ground**, in **the land** of which the LORD **promised** to your fathers to give you.*

*The LORD will **open to you His good treasure, the heavens, to give the rain to your land in its season**, and **to bless all the work of your hand**.*

*You shall **lend to many nations**, but **you shall not borrow**.*

*And the LORD will **make you the head** and **not the tail**; you shall **be above only**, and **not be beneath**, if you listen to the commandments of the LORD your God, which I command you today, and are careful to observe them."*

12. <u>**JOSHUA 18:1-3**</u> – *"Now the whole congregation of the children of Israel assembled together at Shiloh, and set up the tabernacle of meeting there.*

    *And the **land** was **subdued** before them. But there remained among the children of Israel seven tribes which had not yet **received** their **inheritance**.*

    *Then Joshua said to the children of Israel: "How long will you neglect to **go and possess (take ownership of) the land** which the LORD God of your fathers has given you?"*

13. <u>**RUTH 2:1**</u> – *"There was a relative of Naomi's husband, **a man of great wealth**, of the family of Elimelech. **His name was Boaz.**"*

14. <u>**1 SAMUEL 17:25**</u> – *"So the men of Israel said, Have you seen this man who has come up? Surely he has come up to defy Israel;*

    *and it shall be that **the man** who kills him, **the king will enrich with great riches**, will give him his daughter, **and give his father's house exemption from taxes in Israel**."*

15. <u>**1 KINGS 10:23**</u> – *"So King Solomon **exceeded** all the kings of the earth for **riches** and for **wisdom**."*

16. <u>**JOB 1:3**</u> – *"His **substance (wealth, affluence)** also was **seven thousand sheep**, and **three thousand camels**, and **five hundred yoke of oxen**, and **five hundred she asses**, and **a very great household**; so that this man was the **greatest** of all the men of the east."*

17. <u>**JOB 42:11-12**</u> – *"Every man also gave him **a piece of money**, and every one **an earring of gold**. So **the LORD blessed** the latter end of Job more than his beginning: for he had **fourteen thousand***

*sheep, and **six thousand camels**, and **a thousand yoke of oxen**, and **a thousand she asses**."*

18. **PSALM 35:27** – *"Let them shout for joy, and be glad, that favor My righteous cause; yes, let them say continually, Let the LORD be magnified, which has pleasure in **the prosperity of His servant**."*

19. **PSALM 112:3** – *"**Wealth** and **riches** shall be **in his house,** and his righteousness endures forever."*

20. **PSALM 118:25** – *"Save now, I beseech You, O LORD, I beseech You, send now **prosperity**."*

21. **PROVERBS 3:9-10** – *"Honor the LORD with **your possessions,** and with the **first-fruits** of all **your increase;** so **your barns** will be **filled** with **plenty,** and **your vats** will **overflow** with **new wine**."*

22. **PROVERBS 8:12** – *"I, wisdom, dwell with prudence, and find out knowledge of **witty inventions**."*

23. **PROVERBS 8:15-21** – *"By me **kings reign**, and **rulers decree justice.***

*By me **princes rule**, and **nobles**, even all the **judges** of the earth.*

***I love those who love me**, and those who seek me diligently will find me.*

***Riches and honor** are with me, **enduring riches** and righteousness.*

*My **fruit** is better than **gold**, yes, than **fine gold**, and my **revenue** than **choice silver**.*

*I walk in the way of righteousness, in the midst of the **paths of justice,** that I may cause **those who love me** to **inherit wealth,** that I may **fill their treasuries**."*

24. <u>**PROVERBS 10:22**</u> – "***The Blessing of the LORD,** it makes you **rich,** and He adds **no sorrow** with it."*

25. <u>**PROVERBS 13:22**</u> – *"A good man leaves **an inheritance to his children's children,** but the **wealth** of the sinner is stored up for the righteous."*

26. <u>**PROVERBS 18:16**</u> – *"A man's **gift** makes room for him, and brings him before **great men**."*

27. <u>**ECCLESIASTES 10:19**</u> – *"A **feast** is made for laughter, and **wine** makes merry, but **money** answers **all things**."*

28. <u>**HAGGAI 2:6-9**</u> – *"For thus says the LORD of hosts: 'Once more I will shake heaven and earth, the sea and dry land; and I will shake all nations, and they shall come to the Desire of All Nations, **and I will fill this temple with glory,**' says the LORD of hosts.*

    *'**The silver is Mine,** and **the gold is Mine,**' says the LORD of hosts. '**The glory of this latter temple shall be greater than the former,**' says the LORD of hosts.*

    *'And in this place I will give **peace,**' says the LORD of hosts."*

29. <u>**MALACHI 3:10-12**</u> – *"Bring **all the tithes** into **the storehouse,** so that there will be **meat in My house;***

    *and try Me now in this, says the LORD of hosts, If **I will** not **open for you the windows of heaven and pour out upon you such Blessing, that there will not be room enough to receive it**.*

*And **I will rebuke the devourer for your sakes**, so that **he will not destroy the fruit of your ground, nor shall the vine fail to bear fruit for you in the field**, says the LORD of hosts;*

*And **all nations will call you 'Blessed', for you will be a delightful land**, says the LORD of hosts."*

30. <u>**LUKE 5:1-11**</u> – *"So it was, as the multitude pressed about Him to hear the word of God, that He stood by the Lake of Gennesaret, and saw two boats standing by the lake; but the fishermen had gone from them and were washing their nets.*

*Then **He (Jesus) got into one of the boats, which was Simon's**, and asked him to put out a little from the land. **And He sat down and taught the multitudes from the boat**.*

*When He had stopped speaking, He said to Simon, '**Launch out into the deep, and let down your nets for a draught.**' But Simon answered and said to Him, 'Master, we have toiled all night and caught nothing; nevertheless **at Your word** I will let down the net.'*

*And **when they had done 'this', they caught a great number of fish, and their net was breaking**.*

*So they signaled to their partners in the other boat to come and help them. **And they came and filled both the boats, so that they began to sink**.*

*When Simon Peter saw it, he fell down at Jesus' knees, saying, 'Depart from me, for I am a sinful man, O Lord!' **For he and all who were with him were astonished at the catch of fish which they had taken;** and so also were James and John, the sons of Zebedee, who were partners with Simon.*

And Jesus said to Simon, 'Do not be afraid. From now on you will catch men (wins souls).' *So when they had brought their boats to land, they forsook all and followed Him."*

23

31. **<u>REVELATION 21:10-21</u>** – *"Then one of the seven angels who had the seven bowls filled with the seven last plagues came to me and talked with me, saying,* **'Come, I will show you the bride, the Lamb's wife.'**

   And he carried me away in the Spirit to a great and high mountain, and showed me **the great city, the holy Jerusalem, descending out of heaven from God, having the glory of God. Her light was like a most precious stone, like a Jasper stone, clear as crystal***.*

   Also she had a great and high wall with twelve gates, and twelve angels at the gates, and names written on them, which are the names of the twelve tribes of the children of Israel: three gates on the east, three gates on the north, three gates on the south, and three gates on the west.

   Now the wall of the city had twelve foundations, and on them were the names of the twelve apostles of the Lamb. And he who talked with me had a gold reed to measure the city, its gates, and its wall.

   The city is laid out as a square; its length is as great as its breadth. And he measured the city with the reed: twelve thousand furlongs. Its length, breadth, and height are equal.

   Then he measured its wall: one hundred and forty-four cubits, according to the measure of a man, that is, of an angel.

   The construction of its wall was of **jasper***; and the city was* **pure gold***, like* **clear glass***.*

   The foundations of the wall of the city were adorned with **all kinds of precious stones***: the first foundation was* **jasper***, the second* **sapphire***, the third* **chalcedony***, the fourth* **emerald***, the fifth* **sardonyx***, the sixth* **sardius***, the seventh* **chrysolite***, the eighth* **beryl***, the ninth* **topaz***, the tenth* **chrysoprase***, the eleventh* **jacinth***, and the twelfth* **amethyst***.*

   The twelve gates were **twelve pearls***; each individual gate was of one* **pearl***.*

*And the street of the city was **pure gold**, like transparent glass."*

~ ~ ~

As *you* "meditate" on *these* "31 PRO$PERITY scriptures" for 31 days consecutively, and then "keep meditating" on *them* month after month…

<u>*I decree and declare over you that:*</u>

*"**NEW FINANCIAL FAVOR** is NOW coming into your life,*
***NEW MONEY-MAKING IDEA$** is NOW coming into your mind,*
***NEW MONEY** is NOW coming into your hands, and*
***NEW WEALTH & RICHE$** is NOW coming into your accounts!*

***In JEU Mighty Name,** AMEN (And $o Be it)!"*

"His PROPHET, The VOW OF FAITH, And The ANOINTING It Releases For Your Miracle!"

Earlier today *I made a "vow of faith" to the Lord "at the word" of one of "His prophets", and I didn't wake up this Sunday morning intending to make this particular "vow of faith" either!*

But after "His prophet" delivered a "powerful prophetic word and teaching" that spoke to my heart and my situation *[and then he challenged the people to make a "vow of faith" to the Lord],* **I just felt impressed by the Holy Spirit that I was one of the ones who was supposed to partake in that "corporate vow of faith" and "miracle anointing" that was being released at that time!**

Through *"anointed"* preaching of the Word *(which means the prophet preached exactly what God instructed him to preach that day),* suddenly, the "windows of heaven" were "opened" and God was able to "pour out a special blessing" upon His people!

And then **God** *[through His prophet]* **gave His people "an amazing opportunity to sow a special $EED (vow of faith) into that miracle anointing under an open heaven" so that they could receive their desired miracles!** And after I *recognized* "this amazing opportunity"

26

for me to receive *my* "desired miracle", I knew that I had to *quickly* get "my $EED" into this *fertile* ground!

For now, the *"specific $EED-amount"* I vowed (at the word of His prophet), and the *"name of the ministry" (soil)* I made my *"vow of faith"* with, is between me and God!

But I will say that, **this particular "prophet of God" is one of the "true Josephs" in the Church today who has gracefully worn the "coat of revelation" upon his life and ministry for many years!** And during this time, *I have been "personally blessed" to not only sit under this prophet's "cutting-edge revelation and teachings", but I've also been able to "sow $EED" into the anointing of Jesus through his ministry on numerous occasions!*

I shared that so *you* don't think that I was suddenly *pressured* or *deceived* into giving my money away to some preacher or false prophet. *The truth is:* **I didn't give my MONEY away to anyone, but I sowed my $EED into the anointing of Jesus through "His prophet" to receive my miracle…there's a major difference between these two!** *In other words, this was "a conscious act of obedience to the Holy Spirit" based on my knowledge and understanding of the Word in this area of Kingdom giving. So just know that "the kid" is not new to this, but I'm true to this level of Kingdom giving! (Selah)*

Unfortunately, "Kingdom Economics" (which involves both *giving* and *receiving* according to Biblical principles) is a subject and revelation that the Body of Christ is *greatly lacking* but is in *great need* of today. However, there's only a few ministers in the Body of Christ today who truly walk in *this* "mantle of revelation" and can teach it correctly to God's people. And by His grace, I am one of those few ministers who the Spirit of the Lord has *anointed* and *sent* to teach *this* "revelation" in these last days! *So he that has an ear, let him hear!*

Listen, there's something extremely powerful that happens when you make a "vow of faith" under a corporate anointing "at the word of a true prophet!" Doing so not only increases your faith, expectation, and capacity to receive more from God, but it also "accelerates" [and "positions" you to receive] the full manifestation of your miracle!

Although the $EED I sowed today *wasn't* a BIG $EED [according to *amount*], but it *was* [according to *measure*]. Both "the vow I made", and "the $EED I sowed on my vow today" was a BIG $EED *to me*, because it definitely stretched my faith and challenged me to trust God at a new level!

And **when I gave** *"at the word of His prophet"*, then these *"rhema"* words were immediately released into my spirit:

> *"Because you have chosen to '***believe My prophet***' and have stretched your faith in both ***making the vow*** and ***sowing on your vow today***, I AM not only going to ***accelerate*** and ***perform*** the 'specific miracle-harvest' you've asked Me for, but I AM also going to ***accelerate*** and ***supply*** all of your 'specific needs' that you've been praying about lately!* **I AM now causing a ***Supernatural acceleration*** of 'My favor, provision, healing, and manifestation of miracles' to come upon your life in this season!"**

Today, you may be *expecting* certain "miracles" that are actually *ready* to be manifested in your life in this season! And *"this prophetic word"* that you are reading right now has been *prepared for you*, and has now *come to you*, for that reason!

You may have "given or sown $EED(s)" in times past, only to see minimum or no results. *But* **"when you 'make' a vow of faith at the word of a true prophet whom God has anointed and sent to you",** **[and when you 'keep' your end of the vow], then the Holy Spirit and the angels will "accelerate your miracle" in a very commanding way!**

That is what the widow at Zarephath did, she made a *"vow of faith"* with the prophet Elijah whom *God* had *sent* to her. In other words, she *"married His prophet"* [by entering into a *"special financial covenant"* with] him that *he* proposed to *her*. Then she followed his instructions, and her and her house did eat many days (a full year) during a time of famine!

That is what *I* did today, and *that* is what *you* must also do—*you* must *"marry His prophet"* that *God sends* to you, and *"host him"* on the Earth when "the opportunity" is *suddenly* presented to you...And "this prophetic letter" has been written to help prepare you for *when* that time comes soon!

In conclusion, here are *two "Kingdom Economic principles" from this teaching* that will quickly raise *"your giving"* to the next level:

1. *God never looks at the "amount", but at the "measure" in which you give or sow!*

2. *When you make a "vow of faith" under a corporate anointing "at the word of one of His prophets" who has been "sent" to you... then God "accelerates" the manifestation of "your miracle!"*

*"Believe **His prophets,** and **you shall prosper!"***
∼*2 Chronicles 20:20*∼

∼*Scripture References:*

- ➤ *Genesis 22:14; 28:20-22*
- ➤ *1 Kings 17:8-16*
- ➤ *Job 22:27-28*
- ➤ *Psalms 76:11-12*
- ➤ *Malachi 3:10*

- ➤ *Mark 12:41-44*
- ➤ *Luke 4:18-19; 6:38*
- ➤ *2 Corinthians 9:6-15*
- ➤ *Philippians 1:6-7; 4:19*

Turn Your Pain Into Passion

And Your Passion Into Pro$perity

No matter what "hardships and pain" *this life* may bring you,

If you can **STAY FOCUSED ON DOING "THAT ONE POSITIVE THING YOU LOVE TO DO** *and* **ARE GOOD AT DOING"**—

Then **"THAT THING, THAT LOVE, THAT GIFT, THAT PASSION"** has the POWER to pull you out of "any negative situation or circumstance" you may be currently facing, and eventually *your life will be made beautiful again!*

~ *Inspired by the amazing story of J.K. Rowling,*

Best-$elling author of the Harry Potter book series and global brand.

The Best INVE$TMENT

My Timeline Reads:

*"TO INVEST IN YOURSELF,
IS THE BEST INVESTMENT OF ALL"*

This is the **"liberating truth"** that most of our schools today are *not* teaching *"our youth"*, and it's also *"the vision"* that mainstream media is *not* telling *"the masses!"*

In fact, *many of today's leading educators who are seated at the top of "the education mountain"* hope *"our youth"* will NEVER discover and walk in *"this truth"*, that: **"TO INVEST IN YOURSELF, IS THE BEST INVESTMENT OF ALL"**—so if *"they"* are not teaching *"our children"* the *"truth"*, then *"who"* will? And that's where we as *"the sons of God"* come in!

Therefore *"I"* make an appeal to *"our youth today"* to get a hold of *"this truth"*, because it can *"save"* you from years of despair as a result of making *"the wrong investments"* with *your mind, your time,* and *your money!*

In fact, when you get a *firm hold* of *"this truth"* and *"this truth"* gets a *firm hold* of you, *then **you will be empowered to walk in a freedom***

31

that totally disconnects you from "the world system" and will cause you to be in control of your own financial destiny! (Selah)

And now I'm going to shift gears a bit, so I can shed more light on *"this truth"* from a *"Kingdom"* perspective.

Listen: *"To invest in yourself"* is not to imply that you *shouldn't* invest in *"other people's dreams"*, because you *absolutely should!*

In fact, **God will always use the "seeds" you invest into someone else's dreams (first), to bring forth the "harvest" or fulfilment of your dreams at a later time!**

This is *how* **the "Kingdom of God" operates, by a system of exchange— when you give God "seed", He then multiplies it, and gives it back to you as a "harvest".** And the following scripture confirms this principle:

> *"With good will doing service, as to the Lord, and not to men, knowing that* **whatever good (seed)** *anyone does for someone else, he will receive* **the same (harvest)** *from the Lord, whether he is a slave or free." (Ephesians 6:7-8)*

The *"Kingdom of God"* is on the *inside* of every man. And there are *three main ways* **"to sow seed"** *or* **"to invest"** in the *"Kingdom of God" in yourself* and *in others*. It's through investing: **"your time, your special gifts (talents & abilities), and your money".**

The *"Kingdom of God"* is a system, *and* **our Father has set the system up so that ALL of His children can participate and WIN**...But *we* must still be "trained" in how to effectively operate in "His system", so that *we* can *ALL* come out as *WINNER$!*

Always remember: ***THE BEST INVESTMENT OF ALL is when you INVE$T in the "Kingdom of God" IN YOURSELF, and IN OTHERS! And when you INVE$T in the "Kingdom of God" in***

others first, *then* **God will cause people to INVE$T in the "Kingdom of God" in you!**

"And you shall know [this truth], and [this truth] shall make you free!"
∾*John 8:32*∾

The Root of Greed Is A Poverty Mentality

My Timeline Reads:

*"IT'S THE **POOR** WHO ARE **GREEDY,** NOT THE **RICH.**"*

Now before I delve deeper into "this amazing revelation" *by Mr. Robert Kiyosaki*, I will begin by first *"laying a foundation"*. In *this context,* that means: *I will intentionally repeat the "same truths from different angles"* so that I can establish *"a strong foundation to build upon"* as I go forward in this teaching.

It's important to know that a "rich person" can be just as [or more] covetous and greedy than a "poor person" can be. Which leads me to my first foundational point—*defining what it really means* to be a "poor" or "rich" person.

Understand that being "poor" or "rich" has *absolutely nothing* to do with how much "money" a person has or doesn't have, nor does it have *anything* to do with how many "material possessions" (houses, cars, etc.) a person owns or doesn't own. *But being "rich" or "poor" has everything to do with a person's "mindset".*

Therefore, **a person being "poor" or "rich" is not determined by how much money is in their bank account, where they live, or what they drive—but it's determined by their "mindset" and how they have decided to use it.** *(Selah)*

There are many people today who are *rich in manifestation* but are actually *poor in consciousness*—these are individuals who most people *in the world* might label "rich" because their "riches" (nice houses, cars, clothes, etc.) *can* be visibly seen.

And there are many people today who may be *poor in manifestation* but are truly *rich in consciousness*—these are individuals who most people *in the world* might label "poor" because their "riches" *cannot* be visibly seen.

However, **true poverty or wealth can never be measured by what is visibly seen, but by the state of a man's consciousness!** *(Selah)*

Your Subconscious Computer. Your "subconscious mind" works very much like a "computer" works. There are "multiple programs" that have been downloaded into your "subconscious mind" which causes it to perform "specific functions" for you *automatically*.

Likewise with "poverty" or "wealth"—both of these are "mindsets" or "programs" that exist in a person's subconscious mind. And depending on "which program" is currently running in a person's "subconscious mind", will determine what is *automatically* displayed in a person's consciousness and ultimately in their life.

So if you want to change "your financial consciousness" from "poverty to wealth", then you must first change the "current financial programs" in "your subconscious" mind".

Here are a few "sacred cows" that need to be destroyed, or *"very harmful financial programs"* currently existing in the "subconscious minds" of many people today *that desperately needs changing (or, reprogramming)*:

❖ ***"Money is the root of all evil."*** There are many people (even in the Church today) who "misquote" and therefore "misunderstand" the scripture in 1 Timothy 6:10, because they omit *the first four words* that are written. But the scripture clearly states: *"For the LOVE of money is the root of all evil"*—not "money" itself, but the "love" of it. In other words, all the "evil" in a person's life can be traced back to the root, which is, having a "wrong relationship" with money! The "good news" is that *if a person can have a "wrong relationship" with money, then he or she can also have a "right relationship" with money.* And either one of those *"relationships with money" (right or wrong)* will be based on the "financial programs" that are currently running inside of his or her subconscious mind.

❖ ***"I must have a college degree in order to become rich."*** While having a "college degree" can be a major blessing (especially if the education that was obtained in college is usable information in a person's life and career field), but ***some of the world's multimillionaires and billionaires today don't even have a college degree or a high school diploma!*** *(Selah)* This was not said to *discourage* anyone from obtaining either of these two academic achievements—in fact, I *encourage* it, and if you already have either of these two then you should be proud of that—*but the truth is, you don't* <u>need</u> *to have either of these two in order to become rich.* You can become "rich" and make millions of dollars by developing an original idea or product that solves a problem in the lives of many people around the world; or, by modifying an existing product that's already on the market. There are many "constructive ways" you can become "rich", and you don't *need* a "college degree" in order to do it.

❖ ***"I wasn't born with a silver spoon in my mouth."*** *Or, "My parents were never rich so I'll never be rich either."* Listen: just because "your parents or grandparents" were never rich doesn't mean that "you" can't become rich. You may even look at your family up-line (two or three generations) and see that there are "no millionaires" to be found. *But maybe that's because God has called "you" to sit at His feet and study the universal laws of wealth, so that "you" will become **the "first multimillionaire" in your family who breaks the generational "curse of poverty" and releases the generational "Blessing of wealth" upon you and your family.** Have you ever considered that, and if so, then are you up for the challenge?*

As previously stated, the "subconscious mind" works much like a "computer" works—there are multiple software programs downloaded onto the system hard drive, which are all designed to "run automatically" the moment you press the power button on.

But just like a "computer" can have one or more "viruses" that can affect its ability to function properly or at its optimum capacity, so can the "subconscious mind" have one or more "mental viruses" that can adversely affect any area of a person's life, including their finances. When these "mental viruses" are discovered, it's time for some "mental housecleaning and reprogramming".

True wealth is hidden in ideas. And the universe has absolutely "no limit" of new ideas. Here are *three things* that makes *wealthy people* different from most people:

- ❖ *they think of original money-making ideas,*
- ❖ *they fully develop their ideas into new products that are in high demand by consumers,*
- ❖ *and then they place their new products into the marketplace to empower and solve a specific problem in the lives of many people in the world!*

When you focus on using *your* "God-given gifts, talents, and abilities" to *enrich* the lives of many people, then you too will become *rich!*

And this is what Mr. Kiyosaki has masterfully done in creating the *"Rich Dad, Poor Dad"* book series and brand!

Wealthy people are leaders and risk takers. They don't just sit around and wait for "a handout from someone" or for "something good to happen for them"—instead, *they go inside their own mind and make great things happen for them and for the people they are assigned to!*

"Poverty" or "wealth" is *based* on "how you see yourself on the inside", so it all comes down to your own "inner image" and "belief system". *And it's not even so much "your beliefs about money", but it's mainly **"your core beliefs about the value or worth of who you are as a person", and what you are willing or unwilling to do to change your income to make it match your own value of self.***

Every Man Rich. "The poor" are often "covetous" (jealous, greedy) of other people's riches because *they fail to discipline themselves and renew their minds to the "universal laws of wealth and prosperity" that are available to every man.*

However, it's the will of God for "every man" to become "rich" *first* in "consciousness", and *then* in "manifestation". For in doing so, this *positions each man to become "a greater blessing to others", and every man should aspire to become rich for that purpose!*

> *"**Do not be conformed** to this world [system of thinking], **but be transformed by the renewing (or, reprogramming) of your [subconscious] mind;** so that you may prove what is that good, and acceptable, and perfect will of God."*
> ~*Romans 12:2*~

"The More You $OW, The More You SEE!"

*"Bring **all the tithes (seed) into the storehouse,** so that there may be food in My house, and try Me now in this," says the LORD of hosts, "**If I will** not **open for you the windows of heaven and pour out for you such Blessing that there will not be room enough to receive it.**"*
(Malachi 3:10)

When God spoke through "His prophet" to the nation of Israel, saying, ***"I will open for you the windows of heaven and pour out for you such Blessing",*** what that literally means today [for you and I as "believers" and "tithers" under the New Covenant] is that ***He will "open up the eyes of our understanding" and give us "spiritual discernment" or "sight beyond sight".***

This is a higher level of *"sight"* that goes beyond just seeing things on this earth plane *through* "our physical eyes", but it's actually seeing things from God's perspective *through* "our spirit eyes".

As a *"tither"* under the New Covenant, ***your "tithes and offerings" are not "debts you owe" but they are "seeds you sow" into the anointing of Jesus Christ,*** so that you can receive a much greater and richer *"spiritual harvest"*.

*Most believers today who "tithe" have not fully understood this revelation and "Kingdom principle" and how it actually works in their lives— they don't understand that **the "first harvest" they should expect to receive after tithing is not a "physical harvest" but it's a "spiritual harvest". It's when God opens up "your spiritual eyes" and gives you "revelation knowledge and insight"…And the measure in which you "$OW", is the measure in which you are able to "SEE" into the spirit realm.** (Selah)*

That is why you should *always* want to *"give"* MORE than just a *"tithe" (or, tenth)* so that you can *"see"* MORE [in the realm of the spirit]. *And* ***the MORE you can "SEE" in the spirit realm, the MORE you can "have" in the natural realm, if you would only "act" on what you "SEE" in the spirit realm.***

And ***God wants to bring you up to new levels "in your giving" and "in the anointing" where you can not only "SEE for yourself", but you can also "SEE for others" and help point them in the right direction to where their "harvest" is.***

In fact, when you look at the word ***"SEED"*** through Kingdom lenses, you will discover the root word is ***"SEE"***. And why is it so important for you to *know* this truth? *Because **your "$EEDing" (or, $OWing) is directly connected to your "SEEing" revelation knowledge and insight into Heaven's unlimited wealth and resources.** The devil doesn't want you to "$OW", because he doesn't want you to "SEE". Because he knows that your "$EED" contains the "power to get wealth!"*

I've heard numerous of testimonies from *"great men and women of God"* in our day, who after they *"sowed their $EED at certain levels"* in obedience to the Holy Spirit, God then "opened the windows of heaven" and poured out upon them *"uncommon wisdom, superior insight, and money-making ideas"* that matched their level of giving. And then they went on to *"fully develop those God-given ideas"*, thus creating *"new* *streams of massive-passive income"* for their families, ministries, and businesses!

Money is *not* wealth. "Money" is *tangible,* but "wealth" is *intangible. Therefore,* **money comes as a result of first having a wealthy mindset.**

So never focus on "money". *Instead, focus on the **"intangible wealth and resources" that are already resident within your spirit** that can be mined into **"tangible wealth"** in your life. This is accomplished by developing and employing your **"God-given gifts, talents, abilities, and money-making ideas"** to go to work for you.*

Don't be deceived...the *"wealthiest"* people on Earth are *not* the ones who you *see* living in *"mansions"* and driving *"expensive cars".* Again, those *"material things"* you *see* are only the *"results"* that they have first worked with some level of *"intangible wealth".*

But **the wealthiest people on Earth are the ones who are "full of rich ideas", and they know how to turn those rich ideas into "profitable, money-making results" that's a blessing to their lives and to the people they influence.**

Likewise, **"true wealth"** *is sitting on the* **"inside of you"** *right now in the form of* **"rich ideas".** *And as you* **recognize those "rich ideas" and take the time to fully develop them, then you will discover the unlimited power they contain to produce "great riche$" in your life!**

∼ *Scripture References:*

- ➤ *Genesis 22:1-18*
- ➤ *Deuteronomy 8:18*
- ➤ *Psalms 112:3*
- ➤ *Proverbs 8:10-12; 10:22*
- ➤ *1 Kings 3:1-15*
- ➤ *Isaiah 45:3*

- ➤ *Malachi 3:8-12*
- ➤ *Luke 6:38*
- ➤ *2 Corinthians 9:6-10*
- ➤ *Galatians 6:7-8*
- ➤ *Ephesians 1:18*

"The JO$EPH Promotion:

End-Time $upernatural Wealth Tran$fer

For Kingdom Advancement On Earth!"

~*(2018 – 2025)*~

*"Then Pharaoh said to Joseph, 'Inasmuch as **GOD has shown YOU all this**, there is **NO ONE as DISCERNING and WISE as YOU!***

YOU shall be over MY HOUSE, and all MY PEOPLE shall be RULED ACCORDING TO YOUR WORD; *only in regard to the throne will I be greater than you.'*

*And Pharaoh said to Joseph, **'SEE, I HAVE SET YOU** [as a watchman] **OVER ALL THE LAND** (the real estate, resources, and souls) **OF EGYPT!'***

*Then **Pharaoh took HIS $IGNET RING** off his hand and [transferred] it on Joseph's hand, and he clothed him in garments of fine linen and put a gold chain around his neck...*

*Pharaoh also said to Joseph, **'I AM PHARAOH**, and **without YOUR CONSENT no man may lift his hand or foot in all the land of Egypt."** (Genesis 41:39-42, 44)*

42

Here are 5 things Pharaoh bestowed upon Joseph at the onset of his promotion: *great favor, great power/authority, great influence, great responsibility (assignment), and great wealth!*

Therefore, I decree and declare that:

"Over the next seven years (2018-2025), **God is going to Supernaturally transfer wealth into the hands of specific individuals in the Church today—these are His sons who are faithful tithers and sowers into the Kingdom of God** *whom He has personally prepared over the years to use the wealth to finance the end-time preaching of the Gospel to every nation on Earth!"*

This *"***Supernatural wealth transfer***"* is something that *absolutely must take place* in these "last days" *before* the *glorious* **"Rapture of the Church"**—*which is the Destination that all "signs" now point to more than any other time in history!*

At the present time that I am writing this status to you, I am currently reading a book entitled *"***Money Cometh! (To the Body of Christ)***" by Dr. Leroy Thompson, Sr.* He also wrote a companion book entitled, **"Money with a Mission (Putting Your Money To Work In The Body of Christ)"** which also teaches Biblical principles to obtaining wealth for God's Kingdom purposes. Another book worthy of reading is **"Seeding For the Billion Flow"** *by Dr. Bill Winston.*

All three of these books [in one way or another] talk about the *"***end-time Supernatural wealth transfer***" for soul winning and for the advancement of God's Kingdom on Earth.* And there are many more books out there that also expound this same subject, but these are just a few books that came to my mind as I was writing this status today.

In *Dr. Todd Coontz's* CD teaching entitled, **"7 Biblical Wealth Transfers: The Coming Supernatural Wealth Transfer"**, he points out how there has already been "six" major *Supernatural wealth transfers* that have taken place in the lives of Bible patriarchs. They are:

1. ***Abraham*** *(Genesis 12:10)*
2. ***Isaac*** *(Genesis 26:1)*
3. ***Jacob*** *(Genesis 31:6-9)*
4. ***Joseph*** *(Genesis 41:39-44)*
5. ***Israel*** *(Exodus 3:19-22)*
6. ***King Solomon*** *(1 Kings 10:23)*
7. *and* ***"Present-Day You"*** *(Proverbs 13:22 / Psalms 92:10).*

Wow, that *"seventh one"* in particular is definitely something to shout about!—don't you *agree?*

To those of us who have been *"faithful tithers & sowers into the Kingdom of God for many years"* and have allowed the Spirit of God to *"renew our minds"* and *prepare* us for this *"end-time Supernatural wealth transfer"*, you couldn't even begin to imagine the joy and expectation that fills our hearts on a daily basis as we have looked unto Jesus, the Author and Finisher of our faith! *And* ***now the time has come when we are ready to be "major financial distribution centers for God", because that is what He has been preparing us for and desires for us to be on Earth!***

Please note that *"Joseph"* is number four of seven on Dr. Coontz's list of seven Biblical wealth transfers. At another time, I'll share with you some of the amazing *"pro$perity secrets"* from each of these Bible patriarchs on this list. But in *this* teaching, I want to focus on giving you some of the *"wealth keys"* the Lord revealed to me from the life of *"Joseph"*, who [as *Dr. Catherine Ponder* puts it in her book, ***"The Millionaires of Genesis"***] became one of the first *"Billionaires"* of the Bible!

And ***through these five powerful "wealth keys", the Holy Spirit is going to speak to our hearts and show us exactly how to position ourselves as the Church today (both corporately and individually) to*** *be recipients of this great "end-time Supernatural wealth transfer" for the advancement of God's Kingdom on Earth!* So if *you're* ready, then let's begin!

JO$EPH WEALTH KEY #1:
"You Must Become A Problem-Solver In Prison"
～ *Genesis 40:1-8* ～

Whether it's a literal or figurative prison, like Joseph, **you must recognize any opportunity to solve problems with your "God-given gift(s)" even when you may find yourself in a place of deprivation and injustice.**

After Joseph was falsely accused by Potiphar's wife and thrown into prison, he could've very easily hung his head low and cried "Woe is me!" *But instead, Joseph declared his innocence and remained focused on "the prophetic Dream" that was still alive and growing inside of him.*

And because Joseph was a "problem-solver" at heart, he was able to recognize the opportunity to solve a problem with his gift for *two very important men* who were in prison with him. Those two men were the *king's butler* and the *king's baker,* one of which would later connect Joseph to *the king* himself!

Therefore, I decree and declare that:

"Where you are right now, you are able to recognize how **you have been given a golden opportunity to solve a problem with your God-given gift for some very important people!** *And you are NOW solving those problems with precision and excellence, which is NOW preparing the way for you to be connected to a king in your industry who's going to pay you to solve the same problem for him!"*

JO$EPH WEALTH KEY #2:
"Your Gift Will Make Room For You"
∼*Proverbs 18:16*∼

We actually get to see this *scripture fulfilled* in the life of *Joseph*. His *"God-given gift of interpreting dreams"* made room for him and brought him before the king of Egypt, who promoted Joseph and rewarded him *financially*.

Another *scripture* that complements and supports the above *scripture* is found just a few chapters later in the Book of Proverbs. It says:

> *"The king's heart is in the hand of the LORD, like the rivers of water, He turns it wherever He wishes." (Proverbs 21:1)*

Therefore, I decree and declare that:

> *"The heart of a king is right now in the Hand of the LORD, and suddenly, He is going to turn his heart and give YOU uncommon favor with this particular king!"*

*Jesus Christ is "the King of kings and the Lord of lords" (1 Timothy 6:15; Revelation 19:16). And **if there's anybody who knows how to "turn the heart of an earthly king" and give you "uncommon favor" with him, then it would be "King Jesus!"***

King Jesus has the power to give *you* "uncommon favor with *any* earthly king" (no matter *who* he is), in order to accomplish His Father's will and purposes *in their life* and *in yours!*

So as you *"work your gift(s)" as unto the Lord,* trust your King in Heaven to *"make room for you",* and to show you *"uncommon favor"* with *"a king in your field or industry"* who will greatly bless you!

Therefore, I decree and declare that:

*"**Your God-given gift(s) are now** making room for you,
and are now **bringing you in the presence of great
men (a king in your industry)** whom God has given you
uncommon favor with and wealth beyond measure!"*

JO$EPH WEALTH KEY #3:
"The King's Nightmare, Will Cause Your Dream To Come True"
∼ *Genesis 41:1-7* ∼

Remember the old cliché: *"One man's trash, is another man's treasure."* We usually apply this to relationships, but the same principle can also be applied here in Joseph's case: *"The king's nightmare became the golden key that unlocked the prison doors to Joseph's deliverance and the beginning of all his dreams coming true."* In other words, **God turned "one man's nightmare" into "another man's deliverance!"** *(Selah)*

On another note, have you ever thought about what caused *this* "king" to have *these* "nightmares" in the first place—you know, from a *natural* standpoint? Maybe the king partied and drank too much wine the previous night which caused him to have two nightmares in the wee hours of the morning. Although the scripture doesn't denote that "drinking" was the cause of this king's nightmares, but it doesn't say otherwise either. Besides, most kings in those days *did* have a royal cupbearer!

*What if I told you that **the only thing standing between you and "the greatest wealth opportunity of your lifetime" is for a king [in your field of expertise] to have a problem that "only you" can solve, a nightmare that "only you" can interpret!** (Selah)*

Let me also say this: *it wasn't the "devil" who caused the king to have those nightmares either, but it was "God" who troubled the king with those nightmares.* Why? *Because **God knew that when the king had those "nightmares" (which were really "prophetic messages"), they would*** become *"the golden key"* that would unlock the prison doors to Joseph's deliverance and usher him into the palace, which is exactly where He wanted *"His prophet"* to be! *Prophets are assigned to kings.* And we can see *this "Kingdom principle"* all throughout the Bible, and in the relationship between Joseph and the pharaoh of Egypt.

Therefore, I decree and declare that:

*"God is now troubling a king with a nightmare that 'only YOU' can interpret, **a major problem that 'only YOU' are able to solve with your God-given gift and anointing!** And the nightmare (or, trouble) of the king, is the gateway to the fulfilment of your dreams!"*

JO$EPH WEALTH KEY #4:
"You Are Only ONE PERSON AWAY From Your Miracle"
∽ *Genesis 41:9-13* ∽

Even with the internet and social media's ability to market and advertise new and thriving businesses, still *the greatest advertising tool today is done through "word-of-mouth".*

Notice what God instructed *"His prophet"* to do: *"Write the vision and engrave it so plainly upon tablets that **everyone who passes by may [be able to] read [it easily and quickly] as he hastens by."** (Habakkuk 2:2, AMP)*

God is the Originator of the *"word-of-mouth advertising principle"* you see here in this scripture, which is still applied by many people today. That is *when a person (or, people) "catches your vision" and they begin to* **run and tell others** *about it. Or, they begin to* **run and tell people** *how "your gift, product, or service" has solved a problem in their life, and how it can also solve a problem for others!*

*Listen, **you don't need "everyone" liking you…All you need is just "one right person" who likes you! And when that "one right person" likes***

*you, then potentially "everyone who is connected to that person's life"
will like you too…This is not about being liked or disliked by people, but
this is about understanding how the "favor of God" works in a person's life.*

Joseph didn't have any "major industry connections" nor did he have
"access to the internet and social media" like we have today. *But what
he did have is "God's favor" working in his behalf with "one right person"
at "the right time". (Selah)*

The "king" didn't even know "Joseph" personally, and neither did
Joseph know the king. *But Joseph knew "the king's butler" from prison,
who years later "spoke favorably of (highly recommended) Joseph to the
king"* after the king had two very troubling dreams that the butler *knew*
Joseph could interpret! The *"king's butler"* represented that *"one right
person at the right time"* who connected Joseph to his financial miracle.

Therefore, I decree and declare that:

*"Like the king's butler in relationship to Joseph, there is 'a person
who you know right now who is close to a king in your industry'
who has a major problem that only you can solve! And 'this
person' whom you already know will become 'your bridge' that
will connect you to 'the king!' Be encouraged, because **you are
only 'one person away' from walking into a season of the
greatest financial miracles and blessings of your life!"***

JO$EPH WEALTH KEY #5:
*"Uncommon Favor & Wealth Comes through
Solving Uncommon Problems for God"*
∾ *Genesis 41:37-40* ∾

"Favor" comes through solving problems *"for man"*. But *"uncommon
favor"* comes through solving problems *"for God"*. And **when you have
"uncommon wisdom and discernment" working in your life** [like

Joseph did], it will cause you to have "uncommon favor and good success" in the sight of God and man! (Proverbs 3:3-4)

When some people hear the story of how Joseph was *"promoted"* to Prime Minister of Egypt, they tend to focus only on the *"uncommon favor"* that he received through the king and they miss *a very important part of his success.*

Certainly Joseph *did* receive *"uncommon favor and promotion"* through the king, but what some people fail to see is *how **he "paid his dues"** prior to receiving and coming into the "full Blessing" on his life.*

*That's right, **Joseph "paid his dues" not only through the use and development of his gift, but also through the "adversity and trials" that he endured in life while his gift was being developed.** This includes:*

- *jealousy, hatred, betrayal, murder plots, assault, robbery, slavery, malicious lies, false accusations, slander, years of false imprisonment, injustice, abandonment, apathy, etc.*

I'll say it again: ***Joseph "paid his dues"*** *before coming into the "full Blessing" on his life!!! (Selah)*

Also, Joseph didn't just have *"this remarkable gift"* and sit on it, *but **he had a track record of solving problems with his gift for key people at key times.*** This can be clearly seen by *the two dreams he accurately interpreted for **the king's butler** and **baker** years prior to meeting **the king** face to face.* Joseph received "favor and promotion" because he was a "problem-solver" in every environment, *even after being falsely accused and imprisoned for crimes he didn't commit.*

It's important to understand that *Joseph wasn't "promoted" by the king because the king liked his "personality"*—although maybe he did, but *that* wasn't the reason *why* he was promoted. ***Joseph was promoted*** *to the highly-esteemed office of Prime Minister of Egypt **because he was able to*** *solve a major problem for the king of Egypt that none of the other king's men could solve!* And in addition to being "gifted", Joseph also had "great Godly character", which made him a "double-blessing" to the king!

In essence, it was "God" who promoted "Joseph" *through* the "king" to the office of Prime Minister of Egypt, so that "He" would have one of "His prophets" in office to "save many lives" during a severe economic famine! *God strategically placed Joseph in a position of power to solve a specific problem (complete an Assignment) for Him, and he was "compensated handsomely" for doing so!*

<u>*Therefore, I decree and declare that:*</u>

*"God is NOW connecting you to **a king in your industry** (someone of great wealth and power who's in a position to promote you) **who has 'an uncommon problem that only YOU can solve with your uncommon gift and anointing!'** And as you solve this problem for this particular king, he is going to pay you handsomely!"*

<u>**"The JO$EPH Promotion**</u>
<u>**and $upernatural Wealth Tran$fer"**</u>
<u>**(A Present-day, Prophetic Prototype)**</u>

Imagine if there was a *"multi-trillionaire tycoon"* in your industry or field of expertise who suddenly decided to contract YOU to work for his Forbes/ Fortune 500 Corporation. And in doing so, he offered to pay YOU *"billions of dollars"* to solve a major problem for him that "only YOU" could solve, and [by God's grace] you were *more than qualified* to solve it! With *your* NEW *promotion,* in addition to *your* NEW and *very lucrative salary:*

❖ *YOU now dress in the finest of **tailor-made garments** and wear **the finest of jewelry;***

❖ *YOU now own and live in **a lavish palace** for you and your family, where male and female servants take care of your estate;*

51

❖ *YOU now own a fleet of **top-of-the line luxury cars** that you can either drive or be driven in;*

❖ *YOU now travel around the world in **your own private jet** for business and for leisure;*

❖ *YOU now eat at **the finest of restaurants** where top chefs from around the world prepare your meals;*

❖ *YOU wake up every day and are blessed to be able to do **your true life's work** that you love doing—that which God has gifted, called, and put you on the Earth to do;*

❖ *YOU have a very flexible work schedule which allows you to spend more quality time [at home or away on **vacations**] **with your family!***

Wow, imagine that! Can you *"see yourself"* living at this level of prosperity and wealth?—because ***if you can "visualize" it for yourself, then it can be "materialized" in your life!***

God is not a respecter of *"persons"*, but He is a respecter of *"faith in His Word and principles"*. Which means, what God did for *"Joseph"*, He will also do for *"you"*, if you can *"believe"* it!

Preparation is KEY to Promotion

Here are *three keys* that unlocked the prison doors to Joseph's deliverance and promotion: *Divine favor, Divine timing, and [you guessed it]* ***Divine preparation…years and years and years of preparation.***

In other words, Joseph was *"highly-trained"* by God in solving a specific problem with *"his unique gift"*. So when the *opportunity* came [*suddenly*] for Joseph to use "his gift" to solve a problem *"for the king"*, he was *ready* for it without delay!

One man of God said it this way: *"Favor is when preparation meets opportunity."*

<u>*Therefore, I decree and declare that:*</u>

"In this season, there's a great wealth opportunity that's coming to you in your field…and **this is not just 'any' opportunity either, but it's 'the one' that you've been praying and waiting for many years to arrive!** *This great wealth opportunity is coming to you SUDDENLY, and you're going to be ready for it when it comes!"*

<u>*A $pace Has Been "Tailor-Made" For YOU*</u>

In this season, **"God's favor has created a space in your field of influence that ONLY YOU (God-in-you) can fill"** as:

- ❖ *the CEO/President of a major corporation;*
- ❖ *the Senior Partner of a top law firm;*
- ❖ *the Dean of an Ivy League university;*
- ❖ *the starring role in a major motion picture;*
- ❖ *etcetera…*

In other words, no one else can fill "this space" except YOU!

<u>*Therefore, I decree and declare that:*</u>

<u>**"God's favor"** *is going to cause:*</u>

- ❖ *YOUR music CD to go platinum;*
- ❖ *YOUR painting to be admired by a top art enthusiast and showcased in elite art galleries around the world;*
- ❖ *YOUR book to become a #1 New York Times Best$eller;*
- ❖ *YOUR movie script to be financed and brought to the silver screen by a top Hollywood film producer and director!*

These are just a few examples of the levels of *"Divine favor, opportunity, and wealth"* that's coming to YOU as a creative talent *"in this season"*… Why? Because YOU are *"ready"* for it!

Remember: Joseph was literally "in prison" when "Divine favor and opportunity" *suddenly* came to him. *Which means,* **it doesn't matter where you are right now (circumstantially or economically), because God knows your address and He knows how to get "the Blessing" to you wherever you are!**

All of this time, you've been "waiting" on God to *send* "the blessing" to you, and God has just been "waiting" on you to "get ready" to *receive* it! So it's not a matter of *whether or not GOD is ready to give you the Blessing,* because *He is* ready, willing, and able—but the real question is: *"Are YOU ready to receive [and maintain] the Blessing that He's ready to give you in this season?"* Are YOU *"ready"* to go from the prison to the *palace, from the bottom to the top!?* Because *"this Blessing"* that God is ready to release from His Hands is coming SUDDENLY…to all those who are *"prepared"* for it!

<u>*Therefore, I decree and declare that:*</u>

"Because YOU (Joseph) are prepared, you are NOW being summoned to the palace for YOUR promotion!"

<u>*"Josephs ARI$E!"*</u>
*"This is a clarion call to **all the Josephs** around the world, I say to you NOW:*

Josephs ARI$E…
arise from the dungeons of despair and injustice that your false accusers and oppressors have thrown you in, and left you in, to die!

Josephs ARI$E…
your gift has made room for you, and it's NOW bringing you before great men!

Josephs ARI$E…
and take your places as kings and priests in the anointing!

Josephs ARI$E…
and walk in the prophetic mantle that your Heavenly Father has tailor-made for your God-given assignment in the Kingdom of God on Earth!

Josephs ARI$E…
your faith has been tried and tested on purpose and with purpose, and NOW you are being promoted to the top level!

Josephs ARI$E…
and take your places:
at the top of the political/government mountain!
at the top of the business mountain!
at the top of the education mountain!
at the top of the entertainment mountain!
at the top of the media mountain!

Josephs ARI$E…
and take your places as apostles, prophets, evangelists,
pastors, and teachers in the Body of Christ!

Josephs ARI$E…
and take your places as husbands & wives, fathers & mothers in the home!
*I NOW summon **every Joseph** around the world to this call…*
Josephs ARI$E!"

*"But as for you, you meant evil against me; **but God meant it for good, in order to bring about as it is this day, to save many people alive. Now therefore, do not be afraid; I will provide for you and your little ones.** And he comforted them and spoke kindly to them."*
∾ Genesis 50:20-21∾

"Believe in the LORD your God, and you shall be established;
believe His prophets, and you shall prosper."
∾2 Chronicles 20:20∾

EPOCHS & STATIONS

Times, seasons, and places matter. Where God places you according to His time, season, and purpose is paramount to the inspiration that flows to you and through you for others. The following are the actual days, times, and places of inspiration for each post in this book.

2015

  1. Wed. Apr. 1, 2015, SD, CA

2016

  1. Tues. Aug. 23, 2016 @ 2:00 AM, SD, CA
  2. Wed. Sept. 28, 2016 @ 8:25 PM, SD, CA
  3. Sun. Oct. 9, 2016 @ 11:00 PM, SD, CA

2017

  1. Tues. Feb. 28, 2017 @ 1:33 PM, SD, CA
  2. Wed. Mar. 1, 2017 @ 10:13 PM, SD, CA
  3. Sun. Mar. 26, 2017 @ 5:31 PM, SD, CA
  4. Wed. Mar. 29, 2017 @ 3:55 PM, SD, CA
  5. Wed. Apr. 5, 2017 @ 7:15 PM, SD, CA
  6. Sun. Apr. 9, 2017 @ 9:55 PM, SD, CA
  7. Sun. Apr. 16, 2017 @ 2:51 PM, SD, CA
  8. Tues. June 13, 2017 @ 5:34 PM, SD, CA

15 OFFICIAL "PROPHETIC DECREE$"
(From this Book)

*"You shall also decide and decree a thing, and it shall
be established for you; and the light [of God's favor]
shall shine upon your path." (Job 22:28)*

Please join me in declaring the following *"prophetic decrees"*, and watch
"the light [or, revelation] of God's favor" shine upon *your path* to wealth
and prosperity!

*** ***Each "prophetic decree" has already been "personalized" for
you to declare!***

~TABLET #3~

1. *** ***I declare the decree:*** *"I AM a covenant-tither who faithfully
    sows 10% of my gross income into the Lord's work, and I know how
    to put a demand on my covenant with God!" (Malachi 3:10-12)*

2. *** ***I declare the decree:*** *"I AM a tither, who is not greedy of
    filthy lucre, but I honor the LORD with my income (money) and
    with the first-fruits of all my increase! This causes my houses and my
    bank accounts to be filled with wealth & riches, and my businesses
    to overflow with NEW money!" (Proverbs 3:9-10)*

3. *** ***I declare the decree:*** *"I AM a tither, who personally knows
    God as 'Jehovah-Jireh', my one true $ource of income! And
    through my sacrificial sowing of $EED into the anointing, God
    [Supernaturally] provides for me in spite of opposing circumstances!"
    (Genesis 22:1-18)*

4. *** **_I declare the decree:_** *"I AM a tither, whom God has given power to get wealth through multiple streams of income, and I tithe systematically and faithfully off of every one of them!" (Genesis 2:10-14; Deuteronomy 8:18)*

∽TABLET #6∾

5. *** **_I declare the decree:_** *"NEW FINANCIAL FAVOR is NOW coming into my life, NEW MONEY-MAKING IDEA$ is NOW coming into my mind, NEW MONEY is NOW coming into my hands, and NEW WEALTH & RICHE$ is NOW coming into my accounts!" (Deuteronomy 28:8; Proverbs 3:9-10)*

∽TABLET #12∾

6. *** **_I declare the decree:_** *"Over the next seven years (2018-2025), God is going to 'Supernaturally' transfer wealth into my hands as a faithful tither; for I am one of 'His sons' who He has personally prepared [over previous years] to use the wealth to finance the end-time preaching of the Gospel to every nation on Earth!" (Genesis 41; Proverbs 13:22)*

7. *** **_I declare the decree:_** *"Where I AM right now, I AM able to recognize how I have been given a golden opportunity to solve a specific problem with my God-given gift for some very important people! And I AM now solving those problems with precision and excellence, which is NOW preparing the way for me to be quickly connected to a king in my industry who's going to pay me to solve the same problem for him!" (Genesis 40-41)*

8. *** **_I declare the decree:_** *"The KING'S heart is in the Hand of the LORD, and at the right time, the LORD is going to give me uncommon favor with a particular king in my field!" (Proverbs 21:1)*

9. *** **_I declare the decree:_** *"My God-given gift(s) are NOW making room for me, and are NOW bringing me in the presence of great men (kings in my industry) whom God has given me uncommon favor with and wealth beyond measure!" (Proverbs 18:16)*

10. *** **_I declare the decree:_** *"God is NOW troubling a king with a nightmare that 'only I' can interpret, a major problem that 'only I' AM able to solve with the unique 'God-given gift(s) and anointing' that He's placed upon my life! And the nightmare (or, trouble) of the king, is the gateway to the fulfilment of my dreams!" (Daniel 2:1-49; Genesis 41:1-14)*

11. *** **_I declare the decree:_** *"Like the king's butler in relationship to Joseph, there is 'a person who I know right NOW who's a personal assistant to a king in my industry' who has a major problem that 'only I' can solve with my God-given gift! And 'this person' whom I already know will become 'my bridge' that will connect me to 'the king!' I AM encouraged, because I AM only 'one person away' from walking into a season of the greatest financial miracles and blessings in my life!" (Genesis 40-41)*

12. *** **_I declare the decree:_** *"God is NOW connecting me to a king in my industry (someone of great wealth and power who's in a position to promote me), and 'this king' has an 'uncommon problem' that 'only I' AM able to solve with my 'uncommon gift(s) and anointing!' And as I solve this 'uncommon problem' for 'this particular king', he is going to pay me handsomely!" (Genesis 41)*

13. *** **_I declare the decree:_** *"In this season, there's a great wealth opportunity that's coming to me in my field…and this is not just 'any' opportunity, but it's 'the one' that I've been praying and waiting for many years to arrive! This great wealth opportunity is coming to me, SUDDENLY, and I will be ready for it when it comes!" (Genesis 41)*

14. *** **_I declare the decree:_** *"God's Favor is going to cause: 'my music CD' to go platinum; 'my painting(s)' to be admired by a top art enthusiast then showcased and sold in elite art galleries around the world; 'my book' to become a #1 New York Times Bestseller; 'my movie script' to be financed and brought to the silver screen by a top Hollywood film producer and director!"* ∼*Declare which one of these [on or off this list] that applies to you. (Psalm 5:12; Proverbs 3:3-4; 18:16)*

15. *** **_I declare the decree:_** *"Because I (Joseph) am PREPARED…I am NOW being summoned to the PALACE for my PROMOTION!"* *(Genesis 41:14)*

"I have written the VISION and made it plain upon TABLETS…
For it will surely come to pass on its appointed day and time!
In JESUS Mighty Name, AMEN (and So Be It)!"
∼*Habakkuk 2:1-3*∼

19 KINGDOM ECONOMIC PRINCIPLE$
(From this Book)

1. Money can either be used for "good" or for "evil", to *save* lives or to *destroy* them. And that's why it absolutely matters "who" has control of the money and the wealth upon the Earth. It's time for "God's people" to have control of the wealth to advance "His Kingdom" on Earth.

2. The *turning point in Joseph's financial life* came when a "king" had a major problem that *only* "Joseph" could solve with his unique God-given gift.

3. "Tithing" is the key to *reverse the curse* of poverty, debt, lack, and limitation, and *release the Blessing* upon your finances.

4. "First generation tithers" *lay a strong financial foundation for their children and grandchildren (second and third generation tithers) to build upon*, so that *they* can walk in even greater levels of prosperity and wealth than that of their parents and grandparents.

5. In order to *prosper in* "the Kingdom of God" (whether it's in business or in another field), the first thing you must do is *partner up with* "God's Word and principles", and then focus on following His instructions.

6. As you "meditate" on the scriptures, you must *see yourself as Adam, Abraham, Isaac, Jacob, Joseph, Moses, Joshua, Ruth, David,*

Solomon, etc.—you must *visualize yourself as the one whom God is blessing right NOW, both financially and materially.*

7. God never looks at the *"amount" (or, quantity)* but at the *"measure" (or, quality)* in which you give or $OW.

    Quality means: the "value or worth" of a thing to you. For example: in $EED-sowing, the quality of a $EED has less to do with *how much* you give, and more to do with the *spirit* in which you give it. *Your* "money-$EED" has to mean something to *you*, before it means something to *God* and He blesses it.

    "Tithing and $EED-sowing" is *a matter of the heart* that should always be motivated by your *love* for God and your *love* for His people.

    "For God so loved the world, that He gave His only begotten Son". Most people think of John 3:16 as merely a scripture on salvation, but it's actually *one of the greatest "Kingdom economic principles"* in the Bible. It *reveals* how we [as New Covenant believers] should give and sow *our* "money-$EED" into the Kingdom of God and His anointing. Notice that *God gave "His only begotten Son". In other words,* **God gave 100% of everything He had without having anything left over.** God gave a "sacrificial Seed" (His Son), and after He sowed "His Seed", He then used "His faith" to call in "His harvest". When *we* learn how to give *in the same Spirit that God gave,* then *we* can *expect* and *know* that He will multiply *our* "$EED" a hundredfold.

8. When you "$OW" or make a "vow of faith" under a corporate anointing *"at the word of one of His prophets who has been sent to you"*…then God "accelerates" the manifestation of *your* "miracle".

9. If you can stay focused on doing "that one positive thing you love to do and are good at doing", then "that *thing*, that *love*,

that *gift,* that *passion"* has the POWER to pull you out of *"any* negative situation or circumstance" you may be currently facing, and eventually *your life* will be made beautiful again.

10. When you invest *your* "God-given gifts, talents, abilities, graces, and anointings" into the Kingdom, you become empowered to walk in a freedom that totally disconnects you from "the world system" and causes you to be in control of your own financial destiny.

11. God will always use the "$EEDS" you invest into *someone else's dreams,* to bring forth the "harvest" or fulfilment of *your own dreams.*

12. The "Kingdom of God" operates by a system of exchange— when you give God *your* "seed" (time, gifts, money), He then multiplies *your* "seed", and gives it back to you as a "harvest".

13. The best investment is when you INVE$T in the "Kingdom of God" *in yourself,* and *in others.* And when you INVE$T in the "Kingdom of God" *in others* [first], then God will cause people to INVE$T in the "Kingdom of God" *in you.*

14. Being *poor* or *rich* cannot be truly measured by a person's "money or material possessions", but by a person's "mindset" and how he or she has decided to use it.

15. Wealthy-minded people think of "original money-making ideas", and then they invest the necessary time to fully develop their ideas into *high-demand products* that they put into the marketplace to empower and solve a problem in the lives of many people.

16. When you "tithe", God opens up the *eyes of your understanding* and gives you *sight beyond sight (or, spiritual insight)* to see "new things" you didn't see before. This includes: "witty inventions"

and "creative money-making ideas" through the use of *your* "God-given gifts, talents, and abilities".

17. Like Joseph in prison, you must recognize any opportunity to solve problems with *your* "God-given gift(s)" even when you may find yourself in a place of deprivation and injustice.

18. Like Joseph, you can come into great wealth by simply being *"Divinely favored and connected to the right person at the right time"*, and being able to "solve a specific problem" for *that* person.

19. 3 keys to "The JO$EPH Promotion" are:

   ❖ Divine *favor,*
   ❖ Divine *preparation,*
   ❖ and Divine *timing.*

So "be *patient,* stay *faithful and focused on the Word,* and stay *ready*", for *your* "JO$EPH PROMOTION!!!"

ABOUT THE AUTHOR

D'Arcy G. Raboteau is a "Seer, Prophetic Writer, and Teacher" in the anointing. As a five-fold minister, D'Arcy has fully embraced his Mantle and Assignment to bring mind-renewal and maturity to the Bride of Christ. This Assignment is mainly accomplished through writing, publishing, and teaching revelation knowledge and principles from the Word of God through books and various teaching platforms.

D'Arcy also carries a special anointing to teach Kingdom economic principles, based on the foundational principle that "the seed" is the way to true financial prosperity and wealth.

D'Arcy is currently the author of three self-published works entitled: The "Posted!" Trilogy (Volumes 1-3), a Facebook phenomenon.

Today he continues on his prophetic journey to share his testimony, and to teach all those who have an ear to hear.

D'Arcy is a native of "Seed-Diego", California, and a life-time citizen and ambassador of the Kingdom of God on Earth.

THE WIDOW AND HIS PROPHET

A Miracle of Provi$ion through Entrepreneurship

*"A certain woman of the wives of the sons of the prophets
cried out to Elisha, saying, 'Your servant my husband is
dead, and you know your servant feared the LORD. And the
creditor is coming to take my two sons to be his slaves.'*

*So Elisha said to her,
'What shall I do for you? Tell me, what do you have in the house?'*

*And she said,
'Your maidservant has nothing in the house but a jar of oil.'*

*Then he said,
**'Go, borrow vessels from everywhere, from all your neighbors—
empty vessels; do not gather just a few.** And when you have come
in, you shall shut the door behind you and your sons; **then pour it
(your oil) into all those vessels, and set aside the full ones.'***

*So she went from him and shut the door behind her and her sons,
who brought the vessels to her; and she poured out.*

*Now it came to pass, when the vessels were full...
Then she came and told the man of God. And he said,
**'Go, sell the oil and pay your debt;
and you and your sons live on the rest.'"***

∾2 Kings 4:1-7∾

OIL VESSELS / BOOKS

By The Author

From *inspired* posts on Facebook,
to an *innovative* book series!

The "Posted!" Trilogy

Captures a total of 86 prophetic words and insights on love, marriage, divorce, remarriage, prophetic dreams, Assignment, Kingdom economic empowerment, and much more!

Your spiritual eyes will be awakened, and your life will be changed forever!

All books are now available for purchase at www.iuniverse.com, or by calling 1-800-AUTHORS.